Riddles for Smart Families

100+ Original Puzzles to Solve Together

Volume One

James A. Kennedy

Book #3 in the *Books for Smart People* series.

First edition printed in December 2020.

BOOKS FOR

SMART PEOPLE

Titles include:

Riddles for Smart People: Volume 1

Riddles for Smart People: Volume 2

Riddles for Smart Families: Volume 1

Whodunits for Smart People

Author's Note

There are three things you need to know before you dive into this book.

ONE: Riddles are always more fun with your family! I highly recommend taking turns being the Riddle Master. That way you get the chance to provide clues, as well as witnesses to your genius when you solve a puzzle. Some of the riddles are quite challenging, so you'll need to work together as a family to solve them.

TWO: All of the riddles in this book are 100% family-friendly. There is no inappropriate content, violence, or language for younger readers.

THREE: All of the following riddles come from my own brain. However, there are 7+ billion people in the world, and I'm not vain enough to think that other writers haven't had parallel ideas. Any similarities are unintentional.

Now, let's get to the riddles!

Strange Stories

Part One

These stories might sound
strange or impossible at first,
but they're totally normal!
Can you figure them out?

You Can Bank on It

Jean-Paul worked as the manager of a large bank. Over the past few months, a group of robbers had started stealing money from a variety of financial institutions in the city.

However, Jean-Paul never spent money on security. He wasn't worried about theft, because he knew that they didn't keep any money at his bank.

How is this possible?

You Can Bank on It

HINT #1:

Jean-Paul's bank was a non-profit organization that you will find in most cities.

HINT #2:

Jean-Paul's bank relied on donors.

HINT #3:

Jean-Paul's bank provided a much-needed service to local hospitals.

ANSWER:

Jean-Paul worked as the manager for a blood bank. A blood bank takes blood donations from healthy people and gives them to those that are injured or sick.

Make a Run for It

Steve was an avid runner who jogged at least four miles every day, rain or shine. He went through several pairs of running shoes every single year.

One morning, Steve was running along at his usual 8:00 minute/mile pace. He looked up and spotted an elderly woman about 20 feet in front of him. The woman was walking slowly and steadily in the same direction as Steve.

Although Steve didn't change his pace, he never passed the old woman on his run.

Why?

Make a Run for It

HINT #1:

Steve didn't like running outside when it was very cold.

HINT #2:

They were both inside a building when this interaction occurred.

HINT #3:

Neither Steve nor the elderly woman was moving forward.

ANSWER:

They were both using treadmills. The elderly woman was walking on a treadmill a few rows ahead of Steve.

The Disappearing Snack

For the first time ever, Anthony's parents took him to the county fair. He was having so much fun! He rode a bunch of different spinning rides and even won a large teddy bear at the ring toss booth.

Anthony's parents bought him something tasty to eat as they walked around the fairground. All of a sudden, it started pouring down rain. Anthony's snack disappeared almost immediately. How disappointing!

What did Anthony's parents buy for him?

The Disappearing Snack

HINT #1:

The treat that Anthony was eating was very sweet.

HINT #2:

The treat came on a stick and was bigger than his head!

HINT #3:

Anthony's tongue was bright blue while eating the snack.

ANSWER:

Anthony's parents had bought him blue cotton candy on a stick. Unfortunately, when cotton candy gets wet, it disappears incredibly fast.

Song and Dance

Tracy was extremely nervous about getting on stage. She knew she had a great voice, but she had never sung anything in front of strangers before. She preferred to sing in the shower.

She walked on stage, legs shaky, and picked up the microphone. She squinted into the audience, glad they were obscured by the bright lights.

As the introduction to the song started playing, she panicked. Her nerves caused her to forget all of the words! What a disaster!

After the song ended and she left the stage, Tracy was surrounded by admirers who complimented her flawless performance.

If Tracy couldn't remember the lyrics, how was she able to sing the song perfectly?

Song and Dance

HINT #1:

Tracy's friends had come with her, and they were all taking turns singing on stage.

HINT #2:

Tracy had picked her song out of a large printed book.

HINT #3:

Tracy didn't need to remember the words, as they were displayed on a small screen in front of the stage.

ANSWER:

Tracy was singing at a karaoke bar with her friends. The words to every song are shown as the song plays, so you don't need to know all the lyrics.

Up, Up, and Away

Griffin let go of the big red balloon, which slowly floated away. He watched its gentle progress up over the nearby mountains. It eventually faded out of sight.

He then sat down with his friend Lottie and they had a lovely picnic. They had packed peanut butter sandwiches, chips, and fresh fruit. It was all delicious!

As they finished their meal, the balloon returned into view and slowly floated back to the ground beside Griffin.

How is this possible?

Up, Up, and Away

HINT #1:

Someone was steering the balloon.

HINT #2:

The balloon was enormous, almost seven stories tall!

HINT #3:

There were four people standing in the balloon's basket.

ANSWER:

The balloon was a hot-air balloon. His friends had paid for a hot-air balloon ride over the mountains, and Griffin came along because it was a lovely day. He had been holding one of the balloon's ropes as they set off.

The Karate Master

Katharine got home from her karate lesson and still had tons of energy to spare. She stood in the hallway and practiced all the different kicks and punches she had learned earlier that day.

While she was fighting an imaginary enemy, she accidentally punched straight through the front door! Her mom was going to be SO MAD.

Although Katharine had caused some serious damage to the door, her knuckles weren't bruised in the slightest.

Why not?

The Karate Master

HINT #1:

Katharine wasn't particularly strong.

HINT #2:

Her house technically had two front doors.

HINT #3:

Katharine could see through the front door, even before she punched a hole in it.

ANSWER:

The wooden front door was open to let fresh air inside, so Katharine had punched through the screen door.

The Treacherous Path

David was hiking along a scenic path in Arizona when he came to a large yellow sign. It said in big, bold letters: "DANGER! There have been several rattlesnake sightings on this route. Trail closed until future notice." He looked at it for a minute, and then carried on along the path.

A few minutes later, he came across a park ranger collecting trash. He waved at the park ranger, who said, "Sir, you're going to have to turn around. Did you not see the sign? There are rattlesnakes all over this area lately!"

David was completely shocked.

If he saw the sign, why was David surprised?

The Treacherous Path

HINT #1:

David had perfect eyesight.

HINT #2:

David was afraid of rattlesnakes and would not have ignored the sign's message.

HINT #3:

David had looked at the sign, but he couldn't understand it.

ANSWER:

David was illiterate, so he could not read the sign's warning.

Crossing the River

It was the week after Christmas, and Margo and Jamie were bored. They decided to go on a long walk around their neighborhood. They put on hats, gloves, and their warmest coats, and then set off on an adventure.

A few blocks from their house, they walked up to a small river that was three feet deep and completely full. There was no bridge to help them cross. However, they made it to the other side of the river without even getting their socks wet!

How is this possible?

Crossing the River

HINT #1:

It was very cold outside, and there was lots of snow covering the ground.

HINT #2:

Margo slipped a little while they were crossing, because the surface was slippery.

HINT #3:

The two children actually walked along the top of the water.

ANSWER:

Since it was winter, the river had frozen solid. They walked along the ice with no problem.

The Soccer Star

Jack was the best soccer player on his team, the Red Rangers. He was a fast runner and he had a very powerful kick that could send the ball to the other side of the field. He was voted "Most Valuable Player" by his teammates three years running.

One day, the Red Rangers were up against a new team in the league, the Green Hornets. They expected to beat the Green Hornets with no issue. However, Jack kept accidentally kicking the ball to the other team!

Why was Jack having trouble?

The Soccer Star

HINT #1:

Jack did not have perfect eyesight.

HINT #2:

The two jerseys looked almost identical, except for their color.

HINT #3:

Jack couldn't tell when a tomato was ripe.

ANSWER:

Jack had red-green colorblindness, which means he perceived red and green as identical colors. He couldn't tell the two jerseys apart.

Rhyme Time
Animals

Each of the following
rhyming riddles suggests
a different animal. Can you
figure out which creature
the poem is describing?

I'm known for hard work
And my bright yellow stripes.
My honey's a perk,
I help plants of all types.

What am I?

I walk along the desert sand,
I like the heat, I think it's grand,
I can last months without a drink.
That's quite a talent, don't you think?

What am I?

Even down on my knees,
I'm the tallest around.
I can eat tops of trees
With my feet on the ground.

What am I?

I'm known for hard work
And my bright yellow stripes.
My honey's a perk,
I help plants of all types.

What am I?

A bee

I walk along the desert sand,
I like the heat, I think it's grand,
I can last months without a drink.
That's quite a talent, don't you think?

What am I?

A camel

Even down on my knees,
I'm the tallest around.
I can eat tops of trees
With my feet on the ground.

What am I?

A giraffe

You should pass me by
As I move through the sea.
I float like a butterfly
And sting like a bee.

What am I?

If you spot me on safari,
Snap a pic! You won't be sorry.
Once you see me hunt in action
You'll say I'm the "mane attraction".

What am I?

Though I don't like to boast,
My bright plumage is stunning.
I'm more vibrant than most
Other birds in the running.
I am easy to spot,
I am blue, gold, and green.
I can't fly very far,
But my feathers I preen.

What am I?

You should pass me by
As I move through the sea.
I float like a butterfly
And sting like a bee.

What am I?

A jellyfish

If you spot me on safari,
Snap a pic! You won't be sorry.
Once you see me hunt in action
You'll say I'm the "mane attraction".

What am I?

A lion

Though I don't like to boast,
My bright plumage is stunning.
I'm more vibrant than most
Other birds in the running.
I am easy to spot,
I am blue, gold, and green.
I can't fly very far,
But my feathers I preen.

What am I?

A peacock

If I'm in the room,
You're avoiding a topic.
You'll find herds of me
In savannas and tropics.
I've got a long trunk
And a set of huge ears.
I'm enormous but gentle
There's no need to fear.

What am I?

I like to hang out with my pack,
I know they always have my back.
To say hello, I might just howl.
Don't mess with me or I will growl.

What am I?

Come swim with me while you're on vacation,
I find fish to eat using echolocation.
I leap over waves, through the ocean I dart,
I'm social and playful, clever and smart.

What am I?

If I'm in the room,
You're avoiding a topic.
You'll find herds of me
In savannas and tropics.
I've got a long trunk
And a set of huge ears.
I'm enormous but gentle
There's no need to fear.

What am I?

An elephant

I like to hang out with my pack,
I know they always have my back.
To say hello, I might just howl.
Don't mess with me or I will growl.

What am I?

A wolf

Come swim with me while you're on vacation,
I find fish to eat using echolocation.
I leap over waves, through the ocean I dart,
I'm social and playful, clever and smart.

What am I?

A dolphin

Joke Corner

Part One

Wow, you've been working
hard on these riddles!
Take a quick break and
enjoy some short jokes.

Why was the girl cranky as she held her rosary?

Why was the woman's stomach glowing after finishing her meal?

What happens if you put a hot dog in the sun?

Why was the busy food critic always complaining?

What's a witch's favorite shape?

Why was the man depressed while petting his pet duck?

Why was the girl cranky as she held her rosary?

She was feeling a little cross!

Why was the woman's stomach glowing after finishing her meal?

She had a light lunch!

What happens if you put a hot dog in the sun?

It starts panting even harder!

Why was the busy food critic always complaining?

He had a lot on his plate!

What's a witch's favorite shape?

A hexagon!

Why was the man depressed while petting his pet duck?

He was feeling down!

Why did the man wrap mesh around his cell phone?

What weapon do pigs like most?

Why did the girl roll in poison ivy?

Why do crabs never cross the road?

What was the French baker's motto?

What do corn farmers say when you give them a nice compliment?

Why did the man wrap mesh around his cell phone?

He was screening his calls!

What weapon do pigs like most?

A ham grenade!

Why did the girl roll in poison ivy?

She made a rash decision!

Why do crabs never cross the road?

They prefer the sidewalk!

What was the French baker's motto?

No pain, no gain!

What do corn farmers say when you give them a nice compliment?

Aw, shucks!

What kind of mat are you always pleased
to see?

Which rock tastes sour?

What do you call it when you do origami with
your eyes shut?

Why did the lunatic sell his car?

Why does orange juice dislike pulp so much?

Why are a wizard's employees so important?

What kind of mat are you always pleased to see?

A welcome mat!

Which rock tastes sour?

Limestone!

What do you call it when you do origami with your eyes shut?

A blindfold!

Why did the lunatic sell his car?

Because it was driving him crazy!

Why does orange juice dislike pulp so much?

They have a strained relationship!

Why are a wizard's employees so important?

He can't do magic without his staff!

Strange Stories

Part Two

These stories might sound
strange or impossible at first,
but they're totally normal!
Can you figure them out?

The Secretary

Although Olivia's job title was "secretary", she actually had her own personal assistant. Olivia did very little scheduling, filing, or paperwork. She never answered her own phone.

In fact, Olivia was one of the most powerful people in her entire organization, and the decisions that she made affected people around the world.

Where did Olivia work?

The Secretary

HINT #1:

Olivia lived in Washington, D.C.

HINT #2:

Olivia had a government job.

HINT #3:

Olivia had been appointed by the current president of the United States.

ANSWER:

Olivia was the Secretary of State for the U.S. government. That position is responsible for foreign affairs and is fourth in the line of succession for the presidency.

The Grand Opening

Tina's mom drove her downtown to see the new building that had just opened. The city had spent a lot of money to ensure that it was modern, practical, and well-constructed.

Tina looked around and couldn't believe her eyes. It had hundreds of stories!

She walked around the building, incredibly impressed. As she was about to leave, Tina noticed that the new building didn't have a single elevator, or even stairs.

How is this possible?

The Grand Opening

HINT #1:

Tina loved to read.

HINT #2:

Tina owned a card that let her use this building as much as she wanted to.

HINT #3:

Tina took several books with her when she left the building.

ANSWER:

The building was the city's new public library. Although it was only one story high, it contained hundreds of interesting stories for Tina to read.

What a Rip-off!

Tessa went into a business and purchased something from the store's cashier. She then walked over to another employee who worked at the same company.

That employee took the item that Tessa had just purchased and ripped it in half!

Tessa thanked the employee and kept walking.

Why wasn't Tessa upset that her recent purchase had been torn in two?

What a Rip-off!

HINT #1:

Tessa expected the item to be ripped up almost immediately.

HINT #2:

Tessa had also purchased a large bucket of popcorn.

HINT #3:

Tessa was excited to see the latest pirate adventure movie.

ANSWER:

Tessa went to a movie theater. She purchased a ticket for the show, then walked over to the ticket-taker, who ripped it in half to show that it had been used.

The Unusual Scent

It was a beautiful summer evening. Stella and Darren were meeting up for their first date, and they decided to have dinner at a restaurant with an outdoor patio.

Before Stella left her house, she considered putting on perfume. She decided against it. Instead, she sprayed herself with a foul-smelling concoction.

Yuck! She wrinkled her nose at the smell of it. But she knew she would appreciate it later.

Why did Stella cover herself with something that smelled unpleasant if she was trying to impress her date?

The Unusual Scent

HINT #1:

Stella needed this spray in order to eat outside without being bothered.

HINT #2:

Stella put on this spray any time she went outside for a long period of time.

HINT #3:

The spray doesn't smell great to humans, but insects find it truly repellant.

ANSWER:

Stella sprayed herself with bug spray. She didn't want to get covered in mosquito bites while they were eating outside.

Fresh Biscuits

Ding! The oven timer went off.

Priya put on the oven mitts and took out a steaming tray of biscuits. She had found a new recipe online and the results looked promising.

Her son Rakesh walked into the kitchen to see what was cooking. He reached out for a biscuit and she batted his hand away.

"Rakesh! Stop! These aren't for us. If you tried one, you would hate it," Priya said. "I know they look tasty, but don't let anyone in the family eat these biscuits."

Why had Priya baked something that she and her son wouldn't enjoy?

Fresh Biscuits

HINT #1:

Priya did not plan to give the biscuits away to anyone outside their family.

HINT #2:

Each biscuit was shaped like a bone.

HINT #3:

They didn't taste very good to humans, but would have tasted delicious to a certain animal.

ANSWER:

She was making homemade dog biscuits for Bruno, the family's German Shepherd.

The Birthday Girl

Alejandra loved having her birthday on December 25th. She got to see her entire extended family, who lived a few hours away, for a big Christmas gathering.

They always made her a giant chocolate birthday cake. Plus, she got double the presents! This year, she was hoping for a new bicycle and some video games.

Alejandra went to sleep excitedly on Christmas Eve, but woke up sweating a few hours later. She was incredibly hot, even without any blankets. Not for the first time, she wished that her family's apartment had air conditioning.

Why was it so warm in December?

The Birthday Girl

HINT #1:

Alejandra was used to hot weather in December.

HINT #2:

Alejandra spoke Spanish.

HINT #3:

Alejandra didn't live in the Northern Hemisphere.

ANSWER:

Alejandra lived in Buenos Aires, Argentina. In the Southern Hemisphere, December is a very warm month.

The Impartial Judge

Sidney worked as a judge. She was known for being tough, but fair.

Although Sidney spent 25 years in the same role, she never ruled any of the people she judged innocent or guilty. She also never set foot in a courtroom.

How is this possible?

The Impartial Judge

HINT #1:

Sidney didn't go to law school.

HINT #2:

Sidney always worked with several other judges.

HINT #3:

Sidney occasionally gave out a perfect 10.

ANSWER:

Sidney was a figure skating judge. After watching a performance, she would give the skater a numerical score.

The Low Score

Marco had just started playing a new sport. He loved it, and he enjoyed spending so much time outside. He practiced every week, and he quickly began to improve.

One day, Marco finished a game with the lowest score he'd ever had. He was elated! He immediately called his friend Freddy to brag about his accomplishment.

Why was Marco happy about getting a low score in the game?

The Low Score

HINT #1:

This game is played outside on a course.

HINT #2:

Marco bought himself a set of clubs in order to play the game.

HINT #3:

For this game, the lower your score, the better.

ANSWER:

Marco was playing golf. Your score is the number of strokes it takes you to land the ball in the hole. Therefore, the lower the score, the more skillful you are.

The Chicken Farm

Enrique decided to start a small chicken farm.
He started off by buying a big red chicken coop
with plenty of room for hens to roam. He also
bought a huge bag of chicken feed.

He then went to his local farm and bought 10
full-grown hens. Each of those hens laid one
large brown egg per day.

If chicks take 30 days to hatch on average, how
many chickens will Enrique have in total after
one year?

The Chicken Farm

HINT #1:

Enrique did not want a large flock of chickens.

HINT #2:

The farmer offered to sell Enrique a rooster, but he declined.

HINT #3:

Without a rooster, the flock of chickens will not grow in size.

ANSWER:

He will have the 10 hens he started with. Without a rooster, the eggs will not be fertilized and turn into baby chicks.

Attack on the Castle

The king and queen were under attack. Their loyal forces protected them the best they could. Unfortunately, two brave knights were lost in the process.

Ultimately, the defending forces were overtaken. After just 30 minutes of battle, the king was knocked down and defeated. The attackers celebrated their victory.

Just one minute later, the king was back upright, completely unharmed and ready for another challenge.

What had happened?

Attack on the Castle

HINT #1:

Although this incident sounds a bit violent, it was actually part of a fun game.

HINT #2:

A bishop and several pawns also were sacrificed to protect the king.

HINT #3:

The king was about two inches tall.

ANSWER:

It was a game of chess. The king was defeated, ending the game, but the players decided to play again immediately.

Word Mentality

Part One

Time for some wordplay!
This section will test
your knowledge of the
English language.

What word can come after all of the following?
- Sun
- 3-D
- Drinking
- Reading
- Magnifying

Take a panda, a grizzly, or a koala. Add the unit of measurement that equals 12 inches. You'll get a word that means you're not wearing any shoes.

What word, with three different meanings, can complete the following sentence?

"Georgia had to _____ her neck in order to see the large _____ perched on top of the construction _____."

What word can come after all of the following?
- Sun
- 3-D
- Drinking
- Reading
- Magnifying

Glasses

Take a panda, a grizzly, or a koala. Add the unit of measurement that equals 12 inches. You'll get a word that means you're not wearing any shoes.

Bear + foot = barefoot

What word, with three different meanings, can complete the following sentence?

"Georgia had to _____ her neck in order to see the large _____ perched on top of the construction _____."

Crane

Take a creature commonly mistaken for a frog. Add a wooden chair you might perch on while you eat breakfast. You'll get a type of fungus.

What word, with three different meanings, can complete the following story?

"Destiny sat on the couch eating chocolate almond _____ and watching her dog Murphy _____ at the squirrel outside. It had run up the oak tree with the rough _____."

Take the part of your body that cats like to curl up on. Add a common spinning toy. You'll get a portable computer that you can take to school.

Which four-letter word can come before all of the following words?
- Ground
- Stage
- Lash
- Pack
- Stroke
- Space

Take a creature commonly mistaken for a frog. Add a wooden chair you might perch on while you eat breakfast. You'll get a type of fungus.

Toad + stool = toadstool

What word, with three different meanings, can complete the following story?

"Destiny sat on the couch eating chocolate almond _____ and watching her dog Murphy _____ at the squirrel outside. It had run up the oak tree with the rough _____."

Bark

Take the part of your body that cats like to curl up on. Add a common spinning toy. You'll get a portable computer that you can take to school.

Lap + top = laptop

Which four-letter word can come before all of the following words?
- Ground
- Stage
- Lash
- Pack
- Stroke
- Space

Back

Take something you should drink plenty of every single day. Add what a lawyer must provide in order to convict someone. You'll get a type of jacket that will keep you dry in a rainstorm.

What word, with three different meanings, can complete the following sentence?

"Just in ____ she got bored on the plane ride, Kristina packed her favorite mystery book: The ____ of the Missing Brief____".

What five-letter word can come before all of the following words?
- Hero
- Market
- Natural
- Star

Take what soccer players do when they kick the ball to one another. Add a city with a harbor where ships load and unload their cargo. You'll get a document that's required to visit other countries.

Take something you should drink plenty of every single day. Add what a lawyer must provide in order to convict someone. You'll get a type of jacket that will keep you dry in a rainstorm.

Water + proof = waterproof

What word, with three different meanings, can complete the following sentence?

"Just in ____ she got bored on the plane ride, Kristina packed her favorite mystery book: The ____ of the Missing Brief____".

Case

What five-letter word can come before all of the following words?
- Hero
- Market
- Natural
- Star

Super

Take what soccer players do when they kick the ball to one another. Add a city with a harbor where ships load and unload their cargo. You'll get a document to visit other countries.

Pass + port = passport

Rhyme Time
Objects

Each of the following
rhyming riddles suggests
a different item. Can you
figure out which thing
the poem is describing?

My face is flat but also round
On your wall is where I'm found.
There are numbers 'round my rim,
They start with 1 and go past 10.
But I am not a clock, you see!
You'll throw sharp objects into me.

What am I?

I dance in the breeze
I flutter and fly
Let go of my string,
I'll fall out of the sky.

What am I?

I go round and round,
Though I'm stuck in the ground.
You'll find me at a fair
Rising high in the air.
Come on, hop on in!
I'll take you for a spin.

What am I?

My face is flat but also round
On your wall is where I'm found.
There are numbers 'round my rim,
They start with 1 and go past 10.
But I am not a clock, you see!
You'll throw sharp objects into me.

What am I?

A dartboard

I dance in the breeze
I flutter and fly
Let go of my string,
I'll fall out of the sky.

What am I?

A kite

I go round and round,
Though I'm stuck in the ground.
You'll find me at a fair
Rising high in the air.
Come on, hop on in!
I'll take you for a spin.

What am I?

A Ferris wheel

I give the sea its famous taste,
And on your table, I am placed.
If something's bland, just reach for me
Or pepper! He's my best buddy.

What am I?

You'll give me a lick
Though I don't taste too good
Onto letters I stick
So they go where they should.

What am I?

From rodents, I derive my name,
But I'm not furry or untamed.
You will not run scared from me,
I plug into your PC.

What am I?

I give the sea its famous taste,
And on your table, I am placed.
If something's bland, just reach for me
Or pepper! He's my best buddy.

What am I?

Salt

You'll give me a lick
Though I don't taste too good
Onto letters I stick
So they go where they should.

What am I?

A postage stamp

From rodents, I derive my name,
But I'm not furry or untamed.
You will not run scared from me,
I plug into your PC.

What am I?

A computer mouse

I start off a lovely shade of green,
But turn orange when I'm grown.
You'll see me around Halloween,
With a smile all of my own.

What am I?

Although I'm a ball
You won't play sports with me.
Knit me into a shawl,
Or a cozy for tea.

What am I?

I have two main colors: yellow and white,
You'll eat me at breakfast, rarely at night.
But don't eat me whole, I'll make a loud crunch!
Crack me and cook me, then you can munch.

What am I?

I start off a lovely shade of green,
But turn orange when I'm grown.
You'll see me around Halloween,
With a smile all of my own.

What am I?

A pumpkin

Although I'm a ball
You won't play sports with me.
Knit me into a shawl,
Or a cozy for tea.

What am I?

A ball of yarn / wool

I have two main colors: yellow and white,
You'll eat me at breakfast, rarely at night.
But don't eat me whole, I'll make a loud crunch!
Crack me and cook me, then you can munch.

What am I?

An egg

Joke Corner

Part Two

Wow, you've been working
hard on these riddles!
Take a quick break and
enjoy some short jokes.

Why couldn't the fisherman catch anything?

Take several people from Helsinki and put them single file. What do you have?

What type of tree gives the best high fives?

Why does it take a dog a long time to finish watching a movie?

What type of street do ghosts like best?

Where do felines model their new clothes?

Why couldn't the fisherman catch anything?

He had a reel problem!

Take several people from Helsinki and put them single file. What do you have?

A Finnish line!

What type of tree gives the best high fives?

A palm tree!

Why does it take a dog a long time to finish watching a movie?

They keep pressing "paws"!

What type of street do ghosts like best?

Dead ends!

Where do felines model their new clothes?

On the catwalk!

What happened when the cow got loose in the factory?

What did the fish say after eating the worm?

What do gardeners say when they clink their glasses together?

Why do tennis players have trouble with their relationships?

What did the cop say when the woman tried to hand him a huge pile of documents?

Why are tables considered very generous?

What happened when the cow got loose
in the factory?

Udder chaos!

What did the fish say after eating the worm?

I'm hooked!

What do gardeners say when they clink their
glasses together?

Shears!

Why do tennis players have trouble with their
relationships?

Love means nothing to them!

What did the cop say when the woman tried to
hand him a huge pile of documents?

"Just the fax, ma'am."

Why are tables considered very generous?

Because dinner is always on them!

Why did the detective avoid working on cases next to cliffs?

Why did the drapes buy a cell phone?

What did the cutlery say to the new spatula?

What do cats put on before a date?

Why was the tennis player asked to be quiet?

Why are mountains hard to surprise with gifts at Christmas?

Why did the detective avoid working on cases next to cliffs?

She didn't want to overlook anything!

Why did the drapes buy a phone?

They wanted to make a curtain call!

What did the cutlery say to the new spatula?

"Knife to meet you!"

What do cats put on before a date?

Purr-fume!

Why was the tennis player asked to be quiet?

He was making a racket!

Why are mountains hard to surprise with gifts at Christmas?

Because they're always peaking!

Strange Stories

Part Three

These stories might sound
strange or impossible at first,
but they're totally normal!
Can you make sense of them?

Precious Metals

Claudia didn't care for jewelry. She never had her ears pierced, so she didn't wear earrings. She didn't like the feel of bracelets on her wrists. When she wore short necklaces, she felt like they were choking her, and when she wore long necklaces, they would always get hopelessly tangled up.

However, one day Claudia started wearing the same piece of jewelry every single day. In fact, she never took it off.

What was it?

Precious Metals

HINT #1:

This specific item of jewelry had great sentimental value.

HINT #2:

The item was something given to Claudia by her husband.

HINT #3:

She wore the item on her left hand.

ANSWER:

After her wedding day, Claudia started wearing a silver wedding ring.

Good Night, Sleep Tight

Dan and Jessica Morris shared a small two-bedroom apartment in the suburbs. Dan was scheduled to give an important sales presentation to his company's CEO the following day, and he was nervous about it.

Because Dan was a light sleeper at the best of times, he decided to take a sleeping pill to help him get some rest. He headed into the bedroom, and Jessica remained in the kitchen, preparing their lunches for the next day.

Ten minutes later, without looking up from chopping vegetables, Jessica knew that Dan was asleep.

How did she know without checking the bedroom?

Good Night, Sleep Tight

HINT #1:

Dan and Jessica got a two-bedroom apartment for a specific reason.

HINT #2:

Jessica and Dan occasionally slept in different bedrooms so that she could get better rest.

HINT #3:

Dan wore nose strips to bed, but they weren't very effective.

ANSWER:

Jessica could hear Dan snoring loudly.

To Ski or Not to Ski

While on vacation, Kevin tried skiing for the first time. Immediately, he was hooked! He bought a bunch of equipment and started to go skiing every weekend that the weather allowed.

However, Kevin hated being cold. He told his girlfriend Judy that he never wanted to travel anywhere where the temperature routinely dropped below 30 degrees Fahrenheit.

How was Kevin able to go skiing if he avoided cold areas?

To Ski or Not to Ski

HINT #1:

Kevin often fell over while he was first learning to ski, but he was never bruised.

HINT #2:

Kevin lived near a large lake, and his friend Brian owned a speedboat.

HINT #3:

Kevin wore a bathing suit while skiing.

ANSWER:

Kevin was going water skiing, not snow skiing. He would practice as long as the weather was warm enough.

The Truck Driver

Dennis loved his job as a long-haul trucker, driving all around America. He would dance along to music, chat with other drivers on the CB radio, and listen to interesting podcasts. He didn't mind the long hours or the solitary lifestyle, and the pay was great.

Dennis often drove between Denver and Salt Lake City on his travels. He avoided one particular road on this route, because it involved driving through a long tunnel under a mountain.

If Dennis wasn't scared of the dark, why did he always choose a different road?

The Truck Driver

HINT #1:

Dennis would have liked to take this route, but it wasn't an option for him.

HINT #2:

Dennis drove an 18-wheel trucker that was about 14 feet tall.

HINT #3:

Dennis had to think about the height of his vehicle when choosing his routes.

ANSWER:

The tunnel on that road was only 12 feet high. Because Dennis drove a huge truck, he wouldn't have been able to drive through the tunnel without scraping the top of the roof off.

The Spelling Bee

Nicole had been preparing for her school's second-grade spelling bee for several weeks. The theme was "Words Starting with E" and included some hard ones like equipment, elliptical, exuberant, and excitable. Her dad had created flash cards to help her practice the trickiest words.

The big day came, and Nicole spelled everything right! But she was very upset, because she ended up in sixth place.

How did Nicole lose the spelling bee if she spelled everything correctly?

The Spelling Bee

HINT #1:

Nicole made it through the first few rounds of the spelling bee.

HINT #2:

Nicole did, in fact, spell something wrong.

HINT #3:

Nicole and her dad had practiced spelling the word "everything" multiple times.

ANSWER:

Nicole spelled the word "everything" correctly in the first round. Unfortunately, she spelled later words incorrectly and was knocked out of the competition.

Out the Window

Late one night, Francisco was walking his toy poodle Fifi around the neighborhood. He walked by his friend Leigh's house and noticed that the lights were on in her living room and the curtains were open.

He looked over and spotted Leigh standing right next to the window. She was looking straight at him. He excitedly waved at her. It had been quite a while since they last met up.

Although Leigh had perfect vision, she didn't see Francisco and she didn't wave back.

How is this possible?

Out the Window

HINT #1:

Francisco was standing on the sidewalk, in plain view.

HINT #2:

If it was daytime, Leigh would have seen Francisco immediately.

HINT #3:

Leigh couldn't see anything outside the window due to the lighting.

ANSWER:

It was nighttime, so it was dark outside. The light from Leigh's living room made it impossible to see outside. She was actually looking at her own reflection, not at Francisco.

Spare Time

Katie got out of bed, stretched, and went into the kitchen to make herself some coffee.

Hmm… that's odd, she thought to herself. The time on the coffee maker didn't match the time on her phone's alarm clock. She was sure they had been the same just yesterday.

Katie went into the living room to investigate further. The clock on the wall didn't match the clock on her phone either!

What had happened?

Spare Time

HINT #1:

The time on Katie's phone was correct.

HINT #2:

The time on the phone was exactly one hour ahead of the time on the coffee maker.

HINT #3:

This event happens twice a year in most parts of the world.

ANSWER:

The clocks had moved up an hour due to Daylight Savings Time. Some of her items (phone, computer) had automatically adjusted to the change while others (microwave, oven, coffeemaker, wall clocks) had to be changed manually.

Great Chemistry

The chemistry teacher, Mr. Erlenmeyer, was known for being a very tough teacher. Getting an A in his class was a feat accomplished by few students each year.

Mr. Erlenmeyer told all of the students that they would have a test on Friday. It would be a very difficult one, so they needed to study hard.

He also told them that he would be giving them all the solutions they needed.

If so, why would the test still be challenging?

Great Chemistry

HINT #1:

The class had just learned about mixing different compounds together.

HINT #2:

When he said "solutions", he didn't mean the answers to the test questions.

HINT #3:

The solutions would be in glass beakers.

ANSWER:

Mr. Erlenmeyer planned to give his students several solutions (mixtures of two or more substances) to analyze and identify.

The Thoughtful Gift

Patricia thought long and hard about what to get her friend Anne for her birthday. After much deliberation, she decided that Anne could use a new jacket. Anne currently wore a jean jacket that had several patches and holes.

Patricia went to the store and found a really cool black leather jacket. It was just Anne's size, and would fit her like a glove. Patricia bought the coat, took it home, and wrapped it up.

At Anne's birthday party, Patricia gave her the leather coat. Anne thanked her profusely but said that she was unable to wear it.

If the jacket fit Anne just fine, why couldn't she accept the gift?

The Thoughtful Gift

HINT #1:

Anne thought that the coat looked great.

HINT #2:

Anne was very concerned about animal welfare.

HINT #3:

Anne couldn't accept the coat because it was made of leather.

ANSWER:

Anne was a vegan, which means that she decided not to use any products derived from animals. She couldn't eat a variety of things, including meat and dairy, and she couldn't wear real leather or animal fur.

Word
Mentality
Part Two

It's time for some wordplay!
This section will test
your knowledge of the
English language.

Take the part of the body that contains your brain. Add the opposite of dark. You'll get something that every car has on its front.

What five-letter word can come before all of the following words?
- Math
- Thought
- Shock
- Noon

What word, with three different meanings, can complete the following sentence?

"Vanessa thought that the $10 _____ to enter the state _____ wasn't a _____ price."

Take a delicious sweet golden substance. Add something you'll see in the sky at night if it's not cloudy. You'll get a vacation that newlyweds often take.

Take the part of the body that contains your brain. Add the opposite of dark. You'll get something that every car has on its front.

Head + light = headlight

What five-letter word can come before all of the following words?
- Math
- Thought
- Shock
- Noon

After

What word, with three different meanings, can complete the following sentence?

"Vanessa thought that the $10 _____ to enter the state _____ wasn't a _____ price."

Fare / fair / fair

Take a delicious sweet golden substance. Add something you'll see in the sky at night if it's not cloudy. You'll get a vacation that newlyweds often take.

Honey + moon = honeymoon

Take a tiny horse. Add what a dog wags when it's excited to see you. You'll get a way that you can wear long hair.

What four-letter word can come before all of the following words?
- Mark
- Shelf
- Keeper
- End
- Case

What word, with three different meanings, can complete the following story?

"A storm came in on Halloween night. When Erica realized that a ____ of lightning could hit the metal _____ on her Frankenstein costume, she didn't hesitate to _____ inside."

Take a tasty dairy product that you might spread on toast. Add a small creature that buzzes around your picnic. You'll get an insect with beautiful wings.

Take a tiny horse. Add what a dog wags when it's excited to see you. You'll get a way that you can wear long hair.

Pony + tail = ponytail

What four-letter word can come before all of the following words?

- Mark
- Shelf
- Keeper
- End
- Case

Book

What word, with three different meanings, can complete the following story?

"A storm came in on Halloween night. When Erica realized that a _____ of lightning could hit the metal _____ on her Frankenstein costume, she didn't hesitate to _____ inside."

Bolt

Take a tasty dairy product that you might spread on toast. Add a small creature that buzzes around your picnic. You'll get an insect with beautiful wings.

Butter + fly = butterfly

Take a popular Irish dance. Add the tool you might use to chop down a tree or cut logs in half. You'll get a fun type of puzzle with many different pieces.

What word, with three different meanings, can complete the following story?

"Francis had just put his _____ racquet away when he knocked over the bookcase, causing it to fall over and _____ the winter _____ he had planned for dinner."

Take a container where you put your laundry. Add the event that Cinderella ran away from. You'll get a sport that's an absolute slam dunk.

What four-letter word can come before all of the following words?
- Band
- Ache
- Board
- Phone
- Lines

Take a popular Irish dance. Add the tool you might use to chop down a tree or cut logs in half. You'll get a fun type of puzzle with many different pieces.

Jig + saw = jigsaw

What word, with three different meanings, can complete the following story?

"Francis had just put his _____ racquet away when he knocked over the bookcase, causing it to fall over and _____ the winter _____ he had planned for dinner."

Squash

Take a container where you put your laundry. Add the event that Cinderella ran away from. You'll get a sport that's an absolute slam dunk.

Basket + ball = basketball

What four-letter word can come before all of the following words?
- Band
- Ache
- Board
- Phone
- Lines

Head

Rhyme Time
Grab Bag!

Each of the following rhyming riddles describes a different feeling, natural element, or concept. Can you figure them out?

I'm a delicate sphere
I'm both colored and clear
If you touch me, my dear,
Pop! I will disappear.

What am I?

No one knows what causes me
Or makes me go away.
Hold your breath and count to three,
That might hold me at bay.
Maybe ask someone to scare you,
That might do the trick.
But even after they shout "Boo!"
You might still respond "Hic!"

What am I?

I always go up and I never go down
You will get a new one every year.
Some celebrate me with a cake and a crown,
When I change, you might give out a cheer!

What am I?

I'm a delicate sphere
I'm both colored and clear
If you touch me, my dear,
Pop! I will disappear.

What am I?

A bubble

No one knows what causes me
Or makes me go away.
Hold your breath and count to three,
That might hold me at bay.
Maybe ask someone to scare you,
That might do the trick.
But even after they shout "Boo!"
You might still respond "Hic!"

What am I?

Hiccups

I always go up and I never go down
And you'll get a new one every year.
Some celebrate me with a cake and a crown,
When I change, you might give out a cheer!

What am I?

Your age

I'm on the outside of a snake,
I help you measure as you bake.
I can show you what you weigh,
Just step on me, see what I say.

What am I?

When I am out, it's bright and warm.
I hide away when there's a storm.
Too much of me will turn you red,
I go away when you're in bed.

What am I?

A bright beacon of light
Shines out of my face.
I help sailors at night
Pass a dangerous place.

What am I?

I'm on the outside of a snake,
I help you measure as you bake.
I can show you what you weigh,
Just step on me, see what I say.

What am I?

A scale

When I am out, it's bright and warm.
I hide away when there's a storm.
Too much of me will turn you red,
I go away when you're in bed.

What am I?

The sun

A bright beacon of light
Shines out of my face.
I help sailors at night
Pass a dangerous place.

What am I?

A lighthouse

I am always black and white,
Never shades of gray.
You'll find me in the newspaper
I change from day to day.
Fill up all my tiny squares,
Use ink if you're bold!
Doing me will keep you sharp
Even when you're old.

What am I?

I'm a very tasty treat
Oft found in a cafeteria.
Although I'm nice to eat,
I'm chock full of bacteria!

What am I?

Even when broken, I'm still in one piece.
As you grow up, my size does increase.
You'll give me to someone for whom you pine,
You'll see me as candy, oft saying BE MINE.

What am I?

I am always black and white,
Never shades of gray.
You'll find me in the newspaper
I change from day to day.
Fill up all my tiny squares,
Use ink if you're bold!
Doing me will keep you sharp
Even when you're old.

What am I?

A crossword puzzle

I'm a very tasty treat
Oft found in a cafeteria.
Although I'm nice to eat,
I'm chock full of bacteria!

What am I?

Yogurt

Even when broken, I'm still in one piece.
As you grow up, my size does increase.
You'll give me to someone for whom you pine,
You'll see me as candy, oft saying BE MINE.

What am I?

A heart

Joke Corner
Part Three

Wow, you've been working
hard on these riddles!
Take a break and
enjoy some silly jokes.

How do you wake up a professional card player from a nap?

What kind of boats do academics like most?

When is a log not a log?

Why did the lazy bus driver get fired?

What sound do trains make when they sneeze?

Why didn't the police detective trust the doughnut maker?

How do you wake up a professional card player from a nap?

You poker! (You poke her)

What kind of boats do academics like most?

Scholarships!

When is a log not a log?

When it's aflame!

Why did the lazy bus driver get fired?

He was always cutting corners!

What sound do trains make when they sneeze?

Achoo-choo!

Why didn't the police detective trust the doughnut maker?

His story was full of holes!

Where did the chess player go to buy new chess pieces?

What do you call it when two surgeons work well together?

Why did the watchman lift a siren over his head?

Why did the oak tree have to turn the car around and go home?

How did the billboard communicate with the "For Sale" poster?

Where did the chess player go to buy new chess pieces?

The pawn shop!

What do you call it when two surgeons work well together?

Good co-operation!

Why did the watchman lift a siren over his head?

He wanted to raise the alarm!

Why did the oak tree have to turn the car around and go home?

He forgot to pack his trunk!

How did the billboard communicate with the "For Sale" poster?

Sign language!

What do cars eat their dinner off of?

What kind of mail do knights love to receive?

Where do sailors learn their craft?

Why did the bodybuilder go to the seafood restaurant?

Why was the three-layer wedding cake sad?

What's a cannibal's favorite drink?

What do cars eat their dinner off of?

License plates!

What kind of mail do knights love to receive?

Chainmail!

Where do sailors learn their craft?

An internship!

Why did the bodybuilder go to the seafood restaurant?

He wanted to get more mussels!

Why was the three-layer wedding cake sad?

It was always in tiers!

What's a cannibal's favorite drink?

A handshake!

Strange Stories

Part Four

These stories might sound
strange or impossible at first,
but they're totally normal!
Can you figure them out?

The Collector

Early one morning, while it was still pitch-black outside, a man named Tony drove slowly around a wealthy neighborhood. He tried to be as quiet as possible, to avoid waking up the area's residents.

Tony drove until he spotted something he wanted. Then he stopped, got out of his vehicle, and packed the items into his truck. He took something from almost every single home on the block.

As Tony was working his way through the neighborhood, he passed a police car. The policeman gave him a brief wave and allowed him to carry on.

Why wasn't Tony arrested for theft?

The Collector

HINT #1:

Tony was paid for his work.

HINT #2:

Tony wasn't doing anything illegal.

HINT #3:

Everyone was happy that Tony was taking things from their homes.

ANSWER:

Tony was driving a trash truck. He worked as a sanitation worker, driving around collecting trash and recycling from the neighborhood.

The Wedding Reception

Five-year-old Jeanne was excited to go to her aunt's wedding. Her mother had bought her a pink dress that swished when she walked, and Jeanne loved the sound it made.

When they arrived at the wedding reception, Jeanne couldn't believe her eyes. It was the fanciest hotel she had ever seen! There was a big crystal chandelier, red velvet curtains on the windows, and a large fountain on the left side of the room.

Jeanne couldn't resist getting a closer look at the fountain. It was so impressive. She stuck her hand in the fountain for a second or two, then wiped it on her dress.

Her mom ran over, incredibly upset. "Jeanne, look at your new dress! We'll never get those stains out!"

Why was Jeanne's mother so dismayed?

The Wedding Reception

HINT #1:

The fountain was not just decorative.

HINT #2:

The fountain was part of the dinner buffet for the wedding guests.

HINT #3:

The fountain did not contain water.

ANSWER:

Jeanne's aunt had ordered a chocolate fountain as a dessert option for the wedding guests. Jeanne's dress was not covered in water, but in liquid chocolate.

20/20 Vision

Victor had perfect eyesight, so he didn't wear glasses or contacts. He always aced the reading tests at his annual optometrist visits.

One day, he walked into a building and put on a pair of glasses. He wore them for about two hours, then dropped them in a bin as he left the building.

Why did Victor throw the glasses away?

20/20 Vision

HINT #1:

He only needed the glasses for a short time.

HINT #2:

He would have looked silly wearing these glasses around town.

HINT #3:

The glasses were red on one side and blue on the other side.

ANSWER:

Victor went to a movie that was shown in 3-D, so they were 3-D glasses. He put them in the bin at the end of the movie so that they could be cleaned before the next person used them.

Under Lock and Key

Gary Jenkins earned a living breaking into people's houses. He would come up to the door, get out his tools, and fiddle with the lock until it opened.

However, Gary was never arrested, because he wasn't doing anything illegal.

What was Gary's job?

Under Lock and Key

HINT #1:

The people who owned the houses knew that Gary was there.

HINT #2:

Gary's tool set was provided by his employer.

HINT #3:

People were so glad when Gary arrived to break into their homes.

ANSWER:

Gary was a professional locksmith. When people accidentally locked themselves out of their own homes, they would call Gary to help them get back in.

The Hardworking Cleaner

Rebecca spent all of her time cleaning a large mansion on the edge of town. Most of her day involved cleaning up after Rufus, the family's shaggy white dog. He was a great pet, but he shed tons of fur everywhere!

Although Rebecca worked tirelessly and did a great job, she was never paid a single dime. The family replaced her after five years without a hint of sadness.

Why wasn't Rebecca upset by this rude treatment?

The Hardworking Cleaner

HINT #1:

Rebecca couldn't use stairs, so she spent all her time on the ground floor of the mansion.

HINT #2:

Rebecca needed to be charged regularly.

HINT #3:

Rebecca had wheels.

ANSWER:

The family had named their robotic vacuum Rebecca. After five years, her battery no longer held a charge, so she was replaced.

First Day of School

Pedro was excited for his first day at a new school. He walked into the classroom and sat down at his assigned desk, but immediately realized it wouldn't work for him. His teacher, Mrs. Bagtree, kindly let him sit at her big wooden desk up front until they could find him a new one.

Mrs. Bagtree handed out spiral-bound notebooks to the class and asked everyone to write down a few sentences about themselves to share with the class. Pedro started writing, but the notebook's binding hurt his wrist and he immediately smudged the ink. Drat!

Next, Mrs. Bagtree passed out scissors and colored construction paper. She asked the class to make a paper collage of their family, but Pedro couldn't use the scissors.

Why did Pedro have so many issues?

First Day of School

HINT #1:

Pedro was perfectly healthy and didn't have impaired mobility.

HINT #2:

Pedro also used a special glove to play baseball.

HINT #3:

Pedro couldn't write with his right hand.

ANSWER:

Pedro was left-handed. The desk was designed for right-handed students, so he would have had to lean over to write anything. Left-handed people have a variety of challenges living in a predominantly right-handed world!

Turning the Tables

Rosalind admired the table. It was extremely well-designed. She appreciated the symmetry and the hard work that went into crafting it.

All of the table's many elements came together so beautifully. It had clearly taken a long time to assemble.

She then folded up the table and put it back into her binder.

How is this possible?

Turning the Tables

HINT #1:

Many different people worked on creating this specific table.

HINT #2:

You couldn't eat off of this table.

HINT #3:

You'll see this table in any chemistry class.

ANSWER:

Rosalind was in her school's chemistry lab working on a science experiment. She was looking at the Periodic Table of Elements chart that she had printed out.

A Bright Idea

Estelle went to the store and bought a box of yellow bulbs to brighten up her home. When she got back from the store, she went outside and dug a large hole.

After Estelle finished digging the hole, she got the bulbs and then put them in the ground! She then covered them with dirt so that no trace of them could be seen.

She went back inside and drank her cup of hot tea, satisfied with her hard work.

Why did Estelle bury the bulbs?

A Bright Idea

HINT #1:

Estelle was a keen gardener.

HINT #2:

Estelle had bought the box of bulbs from a garden center.

HINT #3:

The bulbs would be yellow when they were fully grown.

ANSWER:

Estelle had purchased yellow tulip bulbs from her local gardening center. She buried them so that they would grow and sprout into flowers the following spring.

YOU DID IT!!!

Wow, you made it through the entirety of the book. Congratulations! Weaker minds would have given up long ago.

Give yourself a well-deserved pat on the back for completing over 100 challenging riddles. You are a certified Smart Family.

I hope you enjoyed this labor of love!

BOOKS FOR

SMART PEOPLE

Riddles for Smart People: Volume 1
Riddles for Smart People: Volume 2
Riddles for Smart Families: Volume 1
Whodunits for Smart People

Printed in Great Britain
by Amazon

13919150R00092